Anthology
of a Twenty Year Old Soul

Ben Courson

Dedicated to my Dad and Mom:
the greatest and most loving
parents in the world

Contents

Preface

As the title indicates, this is nothing more than an anthology: a collection of various, eclectic writings bound to a single book. Some of the chapters are prayers, others are short stories (all Bible stories retold except one), and others are calls to faith and virtue.

I wrote this when I was twenty (which sounds weird because I still am as I'm writing this) and twenty chapters in this collection seemed appropriate. The purpose of this entire book is to promote faith, courage, hope, godliness, and passion for God.

These writings are not written from my strengths, but from my weakness. So these are statements of faith, predicated on my desperate need to get back up and live out these truths. Each story, encouragement, and prayer is written for you to personalize, as if written from your own soul, not from me. We all share the same need for a loving, awesome, fearsome, forgiving God, and I hope in some way these writings will inspire us to carry our crosses, follow our dreams, walk in the Spirit, and love God more than ever before.

Lord, I pray that You would breathe on each page to inspire our faith in You. You are a God of hope, and we long for Your presence. Thank You for drawing close to us every time we draw close to You. Take us to Your will. Fill us with Your love. Lead us by Your Spirit. Change our lives. In Jesus name, Amen.

One

A New Generation

The world staggers at the brink of destruction as they await their imminent demise. They suffer from the festering wounds of fear and confusion left untreated. Wayfarers ever moving and adrift, they never achieve their desired end. Thirsty and parched, they're screaming inside, but they cannot find a voice to communicate their desperation.

We have what they're looking for. The living water is ours to give. We will show them that there's hope.

We are a new generation fated to shake the foundations of the earth. We are conduits of change destined to transmit restoration to the world. This is our era, and now is our time to arise and shine.

God has put a new song in our hearts, and our voices will resound. We have a platform and we will declare amazing grace. God has put His light within us and its brilliance will not be shrouded. We will aim for God's power. We will not be afraid.

We will cast our apathy into the flames of holy passion. We will repossess our devotion. We will remove the bushel, and our zeal will burn bright. We will proclaim the truth on the hilltops and we will not cower in the face of persecution.

We will refuse the course of the crowd. We will break from the pack. We will run and not grow weary and we will run to win the prize. We will press on with eyes like flints, and we will never turn back.

We will continue the message of our forebears and instill hope within our peers. We'll obtain the baptism of the Spirit and our lives will be a testament to God's unconditional love. We will find the lost. We will lead them through their labyrinth of evils. We will lead them to the Father.

We will never give up. We will never back down. We will unite.

We're a host of light waging war upon the forces of darkness. We're ambassadors of a celestial Kingdom preaching good tidings to the children of men. We're cross-bearers journeying through this life, drawing others to our eternal destination. We're the border of His garment channeling healing virtue to crippled legs and broken hearts. We are water from the rock and loaves of bread broken for empty crowds. We are clay for eyes to see and waves for feet to tread. We are the dawn dethroning the tyrannical rule of night. We are the crash of thunder arousing hearts that are asleep. We are stars flashing for a brighter galaxy. We will shine forth God's love.

Together, we will make a difference. Together, we will change our world.

Two

Morning's Battle

It's 7:00 a.m. and you've just barely opened your eyes. Your mind is stuck somewhere between being asleep and being awake, and you try to distinguish reality from your dreams. Gradually you pull yourself back to the real world and you ponder the day ahead.

Which path will you walk today? You're confronted by the difficult decisions here at the same old intersection: right or left? Live abundantly or just get by? Passion or apathy? Persevere or give up? Faith or fear? Walk or fly?

A demon on your shoulder whispers into your ear, "Will you again take that ridiculous path of faith? I deem you quite mad for even considering it. Must I tell you again what you will find on that road? Giants you cannot beat and battles you cannot win! Walls you cannot breach and mountains you cannot scale! There is no victory along the way of faith.

"But you already know this, don't you? That path is stained with your blood, sweat, and tears. Is it really worth the toil? Will you think sensibly for a moment? Face the truth, dreams don't come true and miracles don't happen. Waves weren't meant for walking and skies weren't meant for flying. Stop aiming so high and running so fast! There is no reward at the end of that road. Besides, if you dare to be passionate about God, what will people think about you? Put a basket over your light, and you'll be fine. Just fit in, do what everyone else does, and you'll be all right. Renounce your dreams and reject His absurd promises. Don't take the risk of giving your life away. Hang onto it. Second best isn't so bad."

A cogent argument indeed. Quite sensible, really. Maybe you should hang onto your life and take the easier road. Maybe second best isn't really all that bad.

But before you ride that train of thought any further, an angel stops you dead in your tracks. He stands on your other shoulder and speaks with a voice both genuine and warm.

"Have you so soon forgotten," he says, "and are you so easily swayed? Haven't I warned you of the lies you would invariably hear each day? Promises of failure, and words which incite doubt and fear. These lies are the gravity which pulls you down from the boundless skies of flight.

"So come! Pick up your cross. Retrieve your dreams. Become a child today. Slay the dragons and ride the setting suns. Run upon the water and mount up with eagle's wings. Aim for the heavenly prize. Live abundantly. Live for eternity and live for today. Let your light shine. Be strong and courageous. Never lose heart. Never settle for less. Step out in faith and persevere for the dawn. Nothing is impossible with God."

The roads are before you. Which one will you take today?

Three

Taking the Risk

This is the life, for sure. They say if you do what you love, you won't have to work a day in your life. Then I guess I haven't really worked a day in my life.

The family business is just so satisfying.

Don't misunderstand me, even when you have your dream job, problems will inevitably emerge; but still, the good outweighs the bad a million to one. I mean, what more could one really ask for? I am a fisherman by trade, and fishing has been my passion for as long as I can remember. I quickly acquired the love of fishing because it has been a joy shared by my family for several generations, and every day I am blessed to enjoy the camaraderie with those closest to me. My brother and I, competitive by nature, preserve the thrill of our work through the daily throwing down of the gauntlet - 'I'll win by a landslide today. I'll beat you by at least ten fish . . .' And so we're driven to hard work. We never lay a price on the bet though . . . the bliss of victory is enough.

Family, friends, fishing, the beach, and getting a tan . . . it definitely doesn't get much better than this, and I don't want things to change. I bet I'll be here for the rest of my days, and I wouldn't have it any other way.

These were my musings on that sunny afternoon so many years ago. I remember it well. I am now an old man and not long for this world, and my memory slowly fades with age, but that was a day I will never forget. That was the day my world was turned completely upside down . . .

So there I was, sitting inside our boat (which was now close to shore) happily lost in my thoughts. I absentmindedly examined my fishing net for possible tears, while my brother and father sat beside me also inspecting and repairing theirs.

All of a sudden, as if some inaudible voice told me to look up, I involuntarily lifted my eyes and I saw a Man walking toward our boat. His strides were long and deliberate, and He wore an endearing smile. He took a few steps into the sea so that the water swirled around His ankles. He stood only a few feet from our boat and looked at my brother and me with a gaze piercing and warm.

I looked at the Man and, after a moment, I recognized Him.

This is Jesus of Nazareth! This is the Man reputed to be that Prophet foretold by Moses. People say He is the last hope for the Jews. They say that He is the promised

21

Savior.

I could hardly believe it, but there He stood, looking right at us.

There was a certain mysterious and awesome quality about Him. His presence emanated an abundance of life: joy and sorrow, gravity and mirth, strength and brokenness. It seemed to me that He lacked nothing. And at that very moment, as crazy as it sounds, I in some way became aware that my future was in His hands. I'm not sure how, but I just knew that I was destined to be His disciple.

"Follow Me," He said, "and I will make you fishers of men."

His gracious words were astounding. He was calling me to a life of eternal significance and a life at His side. How could I ever refuse Him? He had instantly caught my heart as if by some invisible hook and was quickly reeling me in.

I glanced over at my brother, and he

slowly nodded as if he too felt his heart being pulled by the Savior. We stood to our feet and dropped our nets.

But just as I rose, reality sunk in.

Are you insane? Are you really going to abandon everything you know and love? Why would you seek a new life when you love your life just as it is? And what if people are mistaken? What if He isn't a savior at all? What if you're just throwing your life away? Will you do that so rashly? You've lost your mind.

Cynicism and objection raced through my mind as I stood deliberating. I looked on Him once more, and His face was beaming. It was as if He knew my struggle . . . as if He knew I would overcome reason and take the leap of faith. He stood there like a king, His brown eyes radiating assurance and grace.

If I don't take this risk, I will regret it forever.

He raised a beckoning hand.

I made up my mind.

I climbed out of the boat after my brother. We knelt on the sand together, and pledged ourselves to the Messiah.

That was the day I decided to follow Jesus, and I have never turned back.

Since my decision for Christ, the enemies of the Gospel have tried to silence me, but I cannot stop talking about my Lord. In Jerusalem they tried to poison me, but I did not die. Caesar Nero, determined to annihilate Christianity, ordered that I be put in a cauldron of boiling oil. Though my skin was burned, I did not die. So I was sentenced to a deserted island with other prisoners, and still I am kept alive.

Also, my brother was beheaded and my friends have been killed because of their allegiance to Christ. Many were stoned, some were burnt at the stake, and still others were crucified. Thousands have willingly laid down their lives.

So, here I sit on my favorite rock while I reflect. I'm coming up on my third year as an exile on this island, and I have never been more at peace. Soon I will see my Lord again. Soon I will be reunited with my brothers and sisters. Soon I will wear a crown of life.

I remember when Jesus told me that if I wanted to really know His love, I would have to let go of my life.

If I don't take this risk, I will regret it forever.

I took the risk to follow Jesus and, though the cost was high, I have never regretted it . . . for I am the disciple whom Jesus loved, and His love is better than life.

Four

My Cross to Carry

O my cross, I long to bear you! For this life is only the beginning, but if I bear you, you will bear me to eternity's end. I will shoulder you up my mountain, and I will not turn back. I will carry you to my death, and I will win my freedom. From you I shall never be parted. To you my heart shall be bound.

People say I'm throwing my life away, but they don't know that one day my cross will transform into a crown. My stock is in a market that will never crash. My treasure is beyond the reach of thieves and rust. Where I'm going, the least are the greatest and the last will be first. I'll aspire to the bottom so that in the end I'll be on top. I will lose the world to gain my soul. I'll sow my death to reap a life that never ends. I'll run for last place, and when my course is done, I'll secure the gold medal. I'll take the lowest seat now, but one day, I'll sit upon an everlasting throne. I'll aim to serve everyone here because, when I reach my destination, I'll reign with lords and kings.

To carry as He carried and to live as He lived. To surrender life and to gain it. To suffer and to overcome. To war and to attain peace.

My cross is often heavy and my strength so swiftly wanes, but in just a little while I'll forever rest in Christ's embrace. The road is long and the afflictions are many, yet upon my arrival I will forget all travail. Today tears are shed and laments are sung, but soon all sorrow shall flee at the light of Heaven's grace. So with a cross on my shoulder may my last breath be, that I might awake to an immortal dawn.

My cross is versatile, adapting to

every condition:

When cutting words steal my joy and revenge looks like justice, forgiveness is my cross to carry. When I see the anguished man begging at the freeway exit, compassion is my cross to carry. When a lost soul is mine to find, eternity is my cross to carry. When a boastful word could appease my pleading pride, modesty is my cross to carry. When I can't feel God in my prison, praise is my cross to carry. When I feel the need for haste and control, patience is my cross to carry. When my enemies surround me and fear demands surrender, courage is my cross to carry.

My cross is the birth of my meaning. It is the emblem of my eternity. It is the open door to my destiny.

O my cross, how I long to bear you! For it is not my end you bear, it is my beginning.

Five

More than Conquerors

Heaven is poised and waiting. Today is passing. The line has been drawn, the moment is in your hands, and you'll never have it again.

Life is always moving, so mount it and ride it to eternity. Pull the Kingdom of Heaven down to your world, and bind your heart to its King. Do not swerve from your pledge to excellence. Do not be afraid of your giants. Stand resolved on divine revolution and rebel against what's accepted. Defy unsound ideology and stand for the truth that endures, even if you must stand alone. Run brazenly in the opposite direction and defeat the dictatorial status quo. Wage an ardent campaign against formalistic convention and unveil the secret fervor.

31

Storm the lines of presumption and breach the walls that divide us. Put your heart into the fight and refuse all but victory.

Aim higher. Capture the infinite. Secure the stars.

You're an ambassador appointed to a broken land, bearing tidings of universal freedom for all people. You hold the key to unlock captive souls. Yours is the voice to kindle abiding hope within cold and infirm hearts. There's a song inside of you serving as an undying anthem to shatter the long and wandering silence. A light hides in your deepest chamber, and it can overthrow the mortal shadows long tyrannizing the minds of men. Your enemy fears what you may become.

Victory awaits you. Now rise to your fate.

Summon your courage and lift your eyes. Clutch your shield, brandish your sword, and fly to the front line. Fearlessly engage your opponent and break all defenses. Spurn every insidious thought of surrender and fight until the triumph is consummate.

Relish at last in your beatific encounter with success over your diabolical foes. Observe the riveting scene of routed enemy soldiers stricken with angst under the service of justice. Attribute all commendation to your heroic Captain. Follow your King to the death.

Shine your light and the darkness will retreat. Fill Heaven, and hell will be empty. Defend good, and evil will withdraw. Fall at the cross, and you will stand on eternity. Seize faith, and despair's iron fist will retract. Worship with joy, and in perfect time, your sorrow will dissipate. Feed your passion, and apathy will starve to death. Keep love alive, and hatred will die. Crown purity, and the devil will be dethroned. Fix your eyes on God, and the world cannot allure your focus. Build God's Kingdom, and Satan's will be razed to the ground.

The battle belongs to the Lord, and in Him, you will conquer.

Six

Faith on the Water

My head swam. My courage fled. My soul writhed beneath the glowering canopy of a starless night. The fight against nature fated us to a bitter end.

The sky was veiled. A growing darkness foreboded a certain doom. Flashes of lightning irradiated great sheets of rain, and towering thunderclouds swelled ominously above us. Swift winds roared in our ears and vigorous billows tossed us unrelentingly. Violent waters crashed into our boat, hastening our inevitable demise. Red in tooth and claw, the sea became to us an invincible tyrant we could not oust.

With bleeding hands and clenched teeth, we pushed hard the nearly splintered oars. Commands were barked only to be lost in the wind. Helpless cries were over-ridden by the perpetual crash of thunder. Tears welled in resigning eyes. Our prospects were quickly fading.

We'd weathered a tempest like this once before, but the Lord was present with us then. Now we are left alone. Surely, we are left alone to our watery graves.

My hope was hanging on a fraying thread, when I thought I saw in the distance a figure walking . . . upon the sea! I thought for a moment I had gone mad, but when I glanced over at the others, their eyes were wild with sudden terror as if they had seen it too.

"Certainly it's a ghost," I thought to myself, "and he bears tidings of death."

The apparition drew near us. I furrowed my brow for a supposed fatal gaze through dark and mist and, to my total amazement, I beheld a most familiar face.

Could this really be the face of my

Lord?

"Now you've lost it," thought I. "First you think you've seen a ghost, now you reckon you see the Lord walking on the water. Your mind is only playing tricks on you. Pull yourself together, and quick!"

But at that very moment, from out of the storm, I heard a voice clear and strong say, "Do not be afraid. Take courage, I am here."

I heard the words and my heart leapt within me. An inexplicable and compelling impulse then overtook me . . .

"Lord," I said, "if it's You, bid me to come upon the water with You."

He flashed an intense smile and said, "Come."

For a moment I studied the turbulent sea while striving to work up the courage to step out. I threw one leg over the edge, and my foot barely met the water before I fearfully lifted it out. My heart raced.

I looked up at Jesus, and His inviting gaze restored my strength. I fixed my eyes on Him, and my foot again met the water. My other foot followed, and I stood firm upon the sea.

I slowly walked toward the Lord, and He to me. We laughed together as we trod victoriously upon the stormy waters. Captivated and overcome, I momentarily forgot the storm around me until out of the corner of my eye I glimpsed a colossal wave hastily approaching me. A howling gale all but struck me down. Fear seized me. I took my eyes off Jesus, and with a shout I sank straightaway.

"Save me, Lord!" I said. And with that, I went under.

No sooner than my descent did I feel a mighty hand grasp my wrist. The Lord lifted me up and took me into His arms.

He looked intently upon me and said, "You of little faith, why did you doubt?"

He carried me back to the boat, and the moment we climbed in, the storm transformed into a perfect calm. The boisterous waters became as clear glass. The wind relinquished its scream. The clouds evanesced and the sleeping sun emerged from behind the mountains.

The Lord stood regal and bright, observing the clearing sky. His eyes flashed with morning light and His countenance shone angelically. A secret beauty issued from Him as if we previewed some future glory.

An overwhelming revelation drove us to our knees. God's Son was in our midst, and we worshipped Him with tears of joy.

And so it was brought home to me: if I will but keep my eyes on Jesus, I can do all things. Because He is on my side, I will pull through the darkest storm. I will endure, and I will know victory.

Seven

Fear

Fear.

Its lies are ceaseless, ever deceiving the hearts of men. Its venomous whispers solidify our weakness. Its thoughts, like bricks laid in our minds, build the wall that separates us from God.

It is the master of every soul. A cold-blooded dictator thieving freedom from its innocent victims. A villain with an iron fist, squeezing valor out of the mightiest of warriors. A slave driver steering our efforts in endless circles until our strength is utterly spent.

Its eyes pierce effortlessly through the brave fronts we contrive, driving our secret wounds deeper still. Its poison pervades our bodies until we lie in the dirt, crippled and motionless. Like a patient hunter, it waits for the perfect moment to strike. We are defenseless flies in its web, hanging in the darkness, awaiting our impending doom.

Its skeletal fingers root out our flowers leaving us only with weeds. Its promises reveal the assurance of winter, but never inform us of spring. Its sky is filled with towering black clouds, intransigently denying the sun passage. Its iron hands play us like lifeless marionettes, pulling every string with sinister precision. Its deluding colors fuse upon our blank canvases, creating a most clever mirage.

It obscures our vision and twists half-truths. It reminds us of all the bad things that have happened, and assures us that they will happen again. It shows what now is, and shrouds the good to come. It forbids the great that could be, and squanders our potentials.

It locks us behind the bars of our

worst memories. It lurks like a shadow behind our darkest dreams. It is the spark igniting our deepest angst, and the small stone initiating the avalanche of our deadliest anxieties.

It is a destroyer. A thief. A liar. A cheat.

And it is calculating. Powerful. Sometimes subtle and inviting. Even generous.

But it is always fatal.

It is a lethal disease capable of bringing down an entire generation one soul at a time.

Yet for all its cunning, fear is not invincible. There is a cure. It can be treated. And the solution is simple.

Courage.

Courage is the sole antidote to this death-dealing toxin, and it alone will heal our infected hearts. It is a certain cure that can foil every subtle and intoxicating stratagem that fear has so delicately devised. It is a cleanser cascading down our deepest emotions, restoring strength to our devitalized faith. It penetrates our souls with its whisper of promise and quickly compels our cowardice to resign its crown.

It fortifies our dreams. It rebuilds our hope. It reminds us that our scars will heal.

It is daring. Audacious. Reckless and heroic. Crazy, yet oddly sensible. Unshrinking, yet somehow small. Strong because of weakness and fierce because of love.

It is the trumpet to fell the highest walls, and a staff to divide the impossible seas. It is a sling to vanquish the strongest giants, and a command to pin the setting sun. It is the soil for a mustard seed of faith, and the word to extirpate the mightiest mountain. It is the broken body to break our chains, and the decision at the crossroads to take the road to the cross. It is the empty tomb to fill our hearts, and the defeat of death to win our souls.

It is the conquest through the Promised Land, and the anthem of Heaven's campaign. It is the embodiment of possibility, and the realization of divine aspiration. It is the eye that beholds the invisible, and the ear that perceives the song of the angels. It is the path to the stars we dream of reaching, and the open gates of destiny.

But courage is not the absence of fear, it is being stronger than fear. It faces fear and looks unflinchingly into its eyes. It understands that fear is a lie, and that it hisses only empty threats. It understands that fear's only intrinsic power is in making us believe it is omnipotent.

But fear has no power.

And so it is in realizing that courage is greater than fear, that fear is overcome.

Eight

Fear Not, Only Believe

I laid my dignity on the line. My need was too great not to. I laid my final prospect at the feet of Jesus.

He was my only hope.

"Jesus," I cried, "my daughter . . . she's . . . she's dying. Come, please come! Lay Your hands on her, and she will live."

He did not speak.

He just looked at me.

I looked deep into His cavernous eyes and read stories of compassion and tales of a deeper power. I saw reflections of healing and images of grace. And then I knew He would answer my prayer.

He affirmed with a slow nod of His head. He smiled reassuringly, beckoned me to follow, and began to walk.

My heart soared. And for the first time in far, far too long, I felt safe. I felt like a child held in the impregnable embrace of a father after wandering through a maze of indifferent streets, trying to find the way home. And in the presence of Jesus, I was home.

I rose to my feet, wiped the tears off my face, and marched proudly behind Jesus.

I was so caught up in the moment that I forgot the vying crowds swarming all around Him. Yet He traveled on with such intentionality and poise that it seemed nothing could hinder Him. Nothing would keep Him from going straight to my daughter. Time was against us, and He knew it.

But when we had nearly arrived, He suddenly halted.

He stopped. We were almost there, and He stopped.

Voices grew quiet. Suspense filled the

air. All was still.

"Who touched Me?" He asked.

His disciples looked curiously at one another, and murmured quietly amongst themselves.

"Master," said one, "what do You mean 'who touched Me?' The crowds are thronging You!"

"No," Jesus said softly, "someone touched Me."

Silence.

Jesus looked at the faces surrounding Him, intently examining each one, when at last a trembling woman crept from behind the multitude.

"Forgive me, Master," she said in a quivering voice, "I am the one who touched You, and I have come with great pain. For twelve years I have been plagued by an issue of blood. I have spent all of my money on physicians, but it has been unavailing. There is no cure for my disease, and it only grows worse with time. So when I heard about the miracles You perform and the legend around Your Name, I thought to myself, 'if I can just touch His robe, then I will be healed.' Please, have mercy on me, and I will be indebted to You forever."

"My daughter," Jesus replied lovingly, "your faith has healed you. Your suffering is over. Go now in peace."

The woman's face beamed bright as the sun. Unable to contain the joy, she ran over to Jesus, kissed His feet, and went her way dancing and singing.

I would have shared her joy, but when I saw three messengers hurrying towards me, my heart began to sink.

Time seemed to slow as one of the messengers opened his mouth to speak.

"Jairus," he said, "don't trouble the Teacher any longer. Your daughter . . . she's dead."

My world collapsed.

My heart stopped. My thoughts fell. My soul was empty. My daughter was dead. And there was nothing I could do.

Time had run out, and Jesus was too late.

My eyes closed. I could not open them. My thoughts wheeled around my head. I could not catch even one. My heart howled but my soul was overrun by a bone-chilling silence. I was lost, meandering through the labyrinth of a slow abyss.

But from the abyss, I heard a voice. From the nothingness, a pale light shone. It began to grow. In the form of words it sparkled and flashed, and the darkness began to disappear. The silence deep within was broken. And in four words, four uncomplicated words, my hope awoke.

"Fear not. Only believe."

The voice belonged to Jesus.

Over and over again it repeated in my head. The words grew from light to strength. And I used that strength to open my eyes and, when I did, I discovered that I had involuntarily fallen to my knees. I looked up at Jesus, and He looked back at me with unwavering eyes. His hand was stretched out as if to say, Take My hand, and I will not lead you to death, but to life.

I accepted that offer.

I stood, set my gaze intently towards my house, and walked on.

But by the time we arrived, my heart again descended to darkness. Many people were crowded inside my house. Weeping and wailing was all I could hear. My house had become hell on earth.

I pushed the mourners out of the way and looked upon my daughter. My beautiful twelve year old daughter.

My lifeless daughter.

I lifted my hand to my eyes despairingly, when I felt a gentle touch on my shoulder. It was Jesus' hand. His simple touch ignited again the soothing words that burned inside my head, *Fear not. Only believe.*

"Why are you all weeping?" Jesus asked. "The damsel is not dead. She is only sleeping."

The crowd erupted in scornful laughter.

Jesus looked around the room, and His piercing gaze seemed to have made even the strongest men afraid. He commanded everyone to go outside, save my family and three of His disciples, and knelt beside my daughter's bed.

He looked upon her, revealing an affection so powerful and so deep that I was brought to tears. There I found a love in Jesus more dazzling and potent than the stars. A love that would never die. A love that could birth new life.

In that moment I opened my heart and locked His eternal love inside. There

His love remains, and there it will always be.

As Jesus took my heart He also took my daughter's hand.

"Little lamb," He said, "arise."

My daughter opened her big brown eyes, and I was complete.

Nine

I Am

I hold your every desire. Everything you're looking for you will find in Me. Come into My presence, just as you are.

I am your Friend. I will rain joy into your cup until it runs over. My Spirit will eradicate the advancing void that has devastated you. I will instill My plans, desires, and dreams inside you, in the place where your swallowing emptiness once lingered. In Me, your purpose will be consummate. In Me, your meaning is complete. My righteous right hand will guide you to hope and fate. We will journey through life together. Together, we will shoulder our crosses and aspire to our heavenly crowns. We will walk on stormy seas today and golden streets tomorrow. We will cross the sweeping fields and attain the mountain summits. The wings of the wind will bear us, and we'll catch the setting sun. I will be with you until the end. I will stick closer than a brother.

I am your Captain. Follow Me, and nothing will be impossible for you. The battle is Mine, and in Me you will be more than a conqueror. We will wage war together. We will fight vigorously. We will be brave and worst our adversaries. We will assail the fortresses of evil and raze the mighty strongholds. We will fell titanic walls with the trumpet. We will slay the giants with the sling. We will draw swords together. We will brandish our spears. We will raise high our heavenly standard. We will emerge victorious. The gates of hell will never prevail.

I am the Author of Creation. I sound the thunderclap as Heaven's applause and I wave My banner of promise and peace among the clouds. The moon I've built for feet to tread and the stars ignite my plans.

I've fashioned the valleys to strengthen you and to the highest mountains I've destined you. I sing my song through the birds and I open the vibrant spring flowers for you. I paint the skies to inspire your flight, and for your goals I've marked the horizon. I'll plant you along distant rivers; your prosperity will come to fruition.

I am a Consuming Fire. I am the light of men, the scintillating flame bearing glad tidings to the captives of darkness. I will vanquish every malicious fear. I will overwhelm every doubt. I will kindle desire within your heart. Your future will crackle with hope. I am the dawn ensuing your darkest night; the soaring sun with healing wings. My face will shine upon you. My splendor will beam through you. Forever your soul will gleam with angelic light.

I am your Savior. I will raise you from the mire that so treacherously ensnares you. I will placate your fiercest storms. My strength hides in your weakness; it will surface in your day of trouble. When you're weary, I will give you power to enterprise every great task. I will carry you through death's shadows to a life that never ends. I pardon your trespasses and cast them into the fathomless seas. My home will be your heart, and your heart will have freedom.

My peace transcends understanding. My grace is infinite. My love is for you.

A love that never dies.

Ten

Pledged to Thee

My weakness for Thy strength
My failure for Thy mercy
My worship to Thy merit
I pledge myself to Thee

My spirit for poverty
My heart for purity
My soul for eternity
Thy cross for my hope

Thy blood is my drink
Thy will is my meat
Thy charity is my breath
Thou hast given life abundantly

Thy favor for my ambition
Thy Word for my vision
Thy grace for my glory
Thou art all my boasting

Anthology of a Twenty Year Old Soul

My heart is a tablet for Thy pen
My hands are instruments for Thy work
My dreams are the desires of Thine heart
I commit my way to Thee
By loss, preservation
By surrender, victory
By death, life
To death I shall trust Thee

In giving I am rich
In fetters I am free
In brokenness I am whole
I surrender wholly to Thee

Thy rod is my comfort
Thy pillar is my guide
Thy promise is my peace
My soul followeth hard after Thee

Thy hand hath been generous
Thy blessings abundant
Thy gifts perfect
Thy face hath shined upon me

Thou art my light in darkness
My sight in blindness

Pledged to Thee

My strong fortress
My help cometh from Thee

Thou art the Prince of Peace
The Author of Faith
The Ancient of Days
My life is Thine forevermore

Thou art the King of kings
The God of gods
The Way. The Truth. The Life.
The Kingdom, the power, and the glory are
Thine

Tho' I be clad in righteous rags
Thou hast prepared Thy table
With Thee I'll dine on that bright day
In merriment and glory

There I'll sit with Abraham
David, Paul, and Peter
For Thy sweet blood is all my worth
Redeemed, the chiefest sinner!

Eleven

Meeting with the King

Come gather 'round, O sons, to hark
And I shall draw speech
from wisdom's well
Come near, ye daughters,
these words to mark
For great is the tale that I shall tell
So come now! and heed the tale
Of my encounter with Christ the True
For I have been behind the veil
And behold! soon you shall go too

At last I arrived. The journey was long and the dangers were many, but I soon forgot all trouble along the way. I had finally reached the palace of the King.

Much time had passed since last I visited, and it was exactly as I remembered it. Yet with wide eyes I beheld afresh its ancient wonders and timeless beauty.

I stood at its grand entrance under two colossal arches, and gazed into the royal hall.

Long shadows swept across the extensive crystalline floor. Great twilit pillars supported the ivory vault above. Slender, pale curtains slept beside vast glass-less windows, swaying idly with the evening breeze. Autumn leaves of brown and orange meandered through, quietly crashing to the floor.

Outside, a weaving river ambled for miles through a rich and pleasant woodland. The scarlet sun was slowly retiring behind the swallowing emerald mountains. A few ignited stars adorned the sky.

Behind one of the windows, a King stood still as stone. His gaze was set upon the distant horizon, and the gleam of dusk silhouetted His imposing stature.

He was tall and strong with a bearing

most dignified. A crown sat atop His head; His hair stirred in the wind. His hands were behind His back, and His feet were planted shoulder's width apart.

At first I thought He didn't heed my arrival, for it seemed He was deep in thought. With nervous anticipation I approached Him. My reverberating footsteps filled the hall. About four paces behind Him, I took a knee reverently.

Without turning, still staring into the distance, He spoke.

"I've been waiting for you." His voice was resonant and wise.

"Yes," I replied, "I am sorry for the delay. I've traveled many miles to come here today, and I've come bearing a heavy burden. It slowed my step and shortened my stride."

For what seemed a lifetime, He made no reply.

My heart began to beat swiftly, and

numerous thoughts raced through my mind.

Then, after I could bear the silence no longer, He turned to face me with a radiant smile.

"And that is why I've summoned you, My old friend," He said with a soft laugh. "For you are heavy laden, and today I shall give you rest. Come now! Let Me rid you of this load."

With one swift motion, faster than the eye could see, He removed the burden from my back.

"Now take My yoke upon you," He said, "for My yoke is easy and My burden is light."

I fell on my face to worship, for my heart was overcome with joy. He graciously accepted my praises and, after a few moments, He took my hand to help me to my feet. He rested His arm on my shoulders, and we walked side by side.

"You bring Me great joy," He said. "I have been seeking one who would worship Me in spirit and truth, as you have done. But you needn't marvel that I've freed you from your load, for I shan't remove just one burden, but any and all! Therefore, cast your cares on Me, for I care for you. And in exchange for your cares, I shall give you life, and that more abundantly.

"Draw close to Me, and I will draw close to you. Humble yourself in My sight, and I will lift you up. For I have searched the whole earth to show Myself strong on behalf of one whose heart is loyal to Me."

We walked in silence for a time as I considered His gracious words. Questions swirled through my mind.

"A long time has passed since last I returned," thought I. "Why have I delayed? In His presence I have found peace, and He removes all encumbrances and cares. What has kept me from this heavenly place?"

My musing was interrupted as we approached a most remarkable throne. Dazzling light emitted from its surface enrobed with shimmering white gold. It stood dignified and proud: an emblem of dominion and justice.

The King slipped His arm from my shoulders, regally ascended a short stair, and sat upon the gleaming throne.

His countenance was holy and worshipful. Equivalently, I felt deeply wicked. Wise was His gaze upon me, and as I stood before Him, my soul felt strangely exposed, naked and open in His sight. His stare was penetrating, as if He was probing into my soul. I could hide nothing. Knowledge was in His eyes, and I was afraid.

"Do not fear," He said at last, "do not fear! I know your sins are many, but I shall remove them all. I shall remove them from you as far as the east is from the west. Only confess your sins, for I am faithful and just to forgive you of your sins, and to cleanse you from all unrighteousness."

I wept and poured out all my heart before Him. I conceded my sins and asked forgiveness. As I confessed to Him, my love for Him intensified, as did my hatred of sin.

"My good son," He said, "your sins are forgiven you, and your iniquities I remember no more. Now walk uprightly, and sin shall not have dominion over you. With every temptation I shall provide a way of escape."

Again I began to worship Him. His countenance radiated like the sun.

"It is true you stand before the King of Kings," He said at length, "but do not be afraid when you approach My throne. This is a throne of grace. Therefore, come boldly, that you may obtain mercy and find grace to help in time of need. I am a very present help in time of trouble, and I shall supply all your need. Delight yourself also in Me, and I shall give you the desires of your heart. Only wait for Me, and let patience have its perfect work, that you may be perfect and complete, lacking nothing.

"Ask, and it will be given to you; seek, and you will find; knock, and the door will be opened to you. When you call upon Me, I will hear you. When you seek Me, you will find Me, when you search for Me with all your heart. Only have faith, for without it you cannot please Me."

"In Your presence, my joy is made full," I said, "and at Your right hand there are pleasures forevermore! But how often will You permit me to come before You? Am I indeed permitted to frequent Your throne?"

"By all means!" He replied gladly. "Come ceaselessly. I reward those who diligently seek Me, and I love to talk with My people. Only . . ."

He was silent for a moment, and His bright eyes darkened to sudden grief. "Only, few journey here now," He said softly, "for faith is difficult to find in these times, and the path one must tread to come here is one of darkness and peril. Too many turn away when they can no longer rely upon their sight. Too many turn away at the first sign of danger. They become angry, slothful, or impatient. When all lights are extinguished and temptations obstruct the way, many turn back.

"But I am well pleased with you, my good and faithful servant!" He continued with renewed cheer. "You have persevered despite the obstacles along the way. But come! Tell Me now of the path you traveled. Tell Me of your journey here."

"I set out alone by night," I said, "and took the road called Straight. It was quite narrow and rather unwelcoming. All about were snakes and beasts and creeping things.

71

Such creatures should give the bravest man a fright! There were also plenty of pitfalls and other such dangers. The sky above was particularly dark, and the stars were veiled. Indeed it was a grueling journey; but when I had finally reached Your palace, all sorrow fell from my heart.

"But I must say, along the way I have been wondering: is there another path one might take? The straight and narrow is the very road I took the first time I met You (and I remember that day well, for it was the day of my salvation). In fact, it has been the only path I have ever taken to come to You. But what of those who've yet to meet You, is there another road, one perhaps less difficult?"

"No," said He, "difficult is the way which leads to life, and there are few who find it. All who come by another way are thieves and robbers. Wide is the gate and broad is the way that leads to destruction, and there are many who go by it."

"Destruction . . . " I shuddered. "You speak of the outer darkness. Where there is weeping and gnashing of teeth, where the worm does not die, and the fire is not quenched."

"Yes," He replied gravely. "How I would have gathered them! How I would have gathered the lost under My wings, as a mother hen gathers her chicks! But they would not, for they love darkness rather than light. All day long I have stretched out My hands to a disobedient and contrary people."

Upon hearing this, a great pain flooded my soul, for I had many friends at home who did not believe. Any previous hope for them now seemed to vanish.

The King beheld my fallen countenance. Pity was in His eyes.

"Take heart!" said He. "Do not despair of any sinner. Do you remember the story of Manasseh, a Jewish king in ancient days? He was the most depraved of all Judean kings; nevertheless, in due time, even he repented his sins. Is My hand shortened at all, that it cannot redeem? Is anything too hard for Me? Let not your heart be troubled, I am able to soften the hardest of hearts! Therefore, go and preach the Gospel to every creature. The harvest is plentiful, and you shall reap if you do not lose heart."

"But who am I that that I should go?" I asked. "I am neither eloquent nor wise. Surely You shall use someone more accomplished than I!"

"Nay," said He, "for I have chosen the foolish things of the world, and the weak things also, to put to shame the wise and the proud. Wherefore, no flesh shall glory in My presence. It is written, 'He who glories, let him glory in the LORD.'"

He arose, descended the stair, placed His right hand upon my left shoulder, and looked directly into my eyes.

"Always remember," He said, "My strength is made perfect in weakness. I shall strengthen you, and help you, and uphold you with the right hand of My righteousness. I shall never leave you. Bear your cross daily, and I shall lead you."

As He assured me with His promises, I discovered empathy and compassion in His eyes. He understood my weakness. Though He was distinguished and assertive, still He was able to sympathize with me.

"Yes," He said solemnly, knowing all my mind. "I have been tempted in all points like as you are, yet without sin. I can be touched by the feeling of infirmity. Come see!"

He held out both His hands, and showed His feet also.

A hole was in each wrist and foot.

"Touch My wounds," He said.

I touched His wounds, and I was made

whole.

"My grace is sufficient for you," He said at last, "and there is healing virtue in My wounds. Ever may you call upon Me, and I will answer. My love knows no boundaries, and My mercy endures forever. Now go, My son, and shine forth this grace to a lost and hurting world."

And with that I went my way with tears in my eyes and a new song in my heart.

So thus it was, and more shall be
For thither shall I soon return
But shalt thou go before the King
His perfect will and ways to learn?
Tho' travel be dreary, shadowed, and long
The destination shall justify the journey
And from your lips shall spring a song
Of the light of grace –
unending; ever burning

Twelve

Heal Us

Save us, Lord. Rescue our generation. We are snared in the net of the devil. You are our only hope.

We have sinned against You and are in danger of judgment. We have abandoned the straight and narrow path. We approach a slow devastation. We hover above the fires of hell. Our time is running out.

Our souls thirst and we reach for salt. With each sin we feed the emptiness we feel, but it never fills. The swelling void consumes us, razing our purpose to the ground.

Our passion and trust are misplaced. Our loyalty is divided. Our lives implode under the weight of our own betrayal.

Our halfhearted lifestyles predicate

the reality of our half dead hearts. We regard our hearts as single, but lead double lives. We let our lips bless God, then kiss the enemy.

We are the blind leading the blind. We are the mute preaching to the deaf. We are the crippled judging the walks of others. Hypocrisy is the cannibal of the body.

We relinquish purity in quest of pleasure. We renounce Your name to promote our own. We betray our first love to go a whoring after other gods. We profess Christ, but our evil works disclose our dead faith. We justify our sins rather than pursuing justification for our souls. We kneel at the cross to obtain counterfeit peace and false security in order to preserve our wicked life-styles under the banner of grace. We drown in our own vomit of decadence and hedonistic depravity. Our trespasses outnumber the stars of heaven; a growing canopy of moral decay stains the sky.

Yet for all our vice and immorality, Your brazen love perseveres through the darkness we create. Your grace over-shadows our darkest atrocities. Your hand reaches across the distance we've run from You. Your mercy expands further than the east is from the west.

Only You can save us, so we cry out to You.

Hide Your face from our iniquities. Stay Your hand and do not punish us in Your hot displeasure. Wash us with pure water and we shall be clean. Absolve our trespasses. We have taken the wings of the morning and we've flown so far from You. Be swift to pursue us. Gather us under Your wings.

Where there is division, remind us that we all wear the same jersey. Where there is war, command us to relinquish our weapons and be our Prince of Peace. Where there is despair, instill in us a courageous, audacious hope.

We are defeated. Win us back to You. We are captives, so speak the truth that sets us free. We're awake to a severe reality, but You can bring us back to our dreams. Fix our aim and be our target. Heal our hearts. Be the strength of our lives. Break our obstinacy and give us hearts like children.

Walk on the waves to rescue our sinking ship. Pass through the crowd and give us a chance to clutch Your garment. Turn water into wine and pour the best of Your Spirit into these final days. Fashion us into vessels of honor and sanctification. Our sins are like scarlet: wash them white as snow. Make Your face to shine on us and let us find grace in Your eyes.

You are the Physician of souls. You are our only hope. Heal us.

Thirteen

Giants of Faith

God searches the earth for hearts fully devoted to Him. Will giants of faith be found in our generation?

God chooses the foolish, the base, the frail, and the despised to transform the world. He calls ordinary people who believe in a power greater than themselves. He summons faithful men who society regards as nothing. He destines regular women to be conduits of change.

Where are the Davids who will determine to know nothing of apathy, and worship with a passion to shake the foundations of Heaven? Where are the Josephs who will hold to the path of purity even when it leads to suffering? Where are the Peters who will dare to be vulnerable and venture the stormy seas?

Where are the Abrahams who against hope will believe in hope, waiting for the promises of God? Where are the Jacobs who will wrestle God for the blessing and prevail? Where are the Joshuas who will have faith to command the sun? Where are the Hannahs who will pray with the fervor that moves God's hand to mercy?

Where are the Marys who will spend tears and treasure on the feet of Jesus? Where are the Gideons who will march to war entirely outnumbered, entrust the battle to the Lord, and emerge victorious despite all odds? Where are the Johns who will have the courage to warn the lost of the everlasting fires?

Where are the Esthers who will relinquish comfort and security for the salvation of God's people? Where are the Daniels who will cherish devotion more than life itself? Where are the Josiahs who will abolish and burn idolatry in the fires of godly zeal? Where are the Jeremiahs who will preach the reality of God's wrath and judgment while contemporaries declare a false peace to assuage the fears of the wicked?

Where are the men who will refuse to kiss the enemy? Where are the women who will seize virtue at the border of His garment? Where are the disciples who will aspire for their crosses? Where are Heaven's ambassadors who will deliver the Gospel of peace to a dying and forlorn world? Where are the warriors who will claim victory and storm hell's strongholds?

Who will fight for our generation?

The eyes of the Lord run to and fro throughout the whole earth to show Himself strong on behalf of those whose hearts are loyal to Him. Will His eyes find you?

Fourteen

Jonah's Second Chance

"Throw me into the sea!" I said. "For I am the cause of this fearsome storm. Throw me overboard and the storm shall cease!"

I was tossed into the ocean. I fell to the heart of the sea. I swayed out of consciousness. I awoke in darkness.

Where am I? How did I come to this place? What is this new terror that has befallen me?

I cannot move and I feel trapped as if in a cage of giant mammal flesh. A horrid nauseating stench mingled with incredible stifling heat swirls around me. Irregular floods of water break against the heavy walls, and small wriggling creatures strike my face. Salty sweat streams down my body as slippery cords coil round my head. An ominous fear lingers in the thick oppressive air of this dark and mysterious chamber.

I can't puzzle out this bizarre situation, and whether I am now living or dead I cannot say. I am lost in confusion and I desperately wish this hard agony would soon relent. Bewilderment and horror drive me steadily toward a mad chasm of mental decay. My frantic thoughts probe for solutions unavailingly and I am left to a slow despair. O doomed fate that I should be bound to such fury!

Yet for all my suffering I cannot complain, for I deserve this great punishment. God commanded me to preach to the Assyrians in Nineveh, but I refused to go. I ran away from Him and rebelled against my calling. The last thing I wanted to do was go to the wicked and barbaric Ninevites, seeing that I have hated them all my life. It was my fear that God would show them mercy if they should turn, but I could not find it in my heart to forgive them of their countless atrocities.

How foolish! How wretched! How miserably I have behaved! At last my unbending defiance has caught up with me. Now I am justly abandoned to face my guilty conscience while my forlorn soul reels at the brink of some wild abyss. My resistance has severed my life from God's plans, and I am compelled to resign myself to this unhappy end. My hard heart has been broken. My destiny is blighted. My faint hope passes into shadow.

I would do anything for another chance, but I'm not sure I have any chances left.

No sooner had the thought crossed my mind than a great and terrible roar sounded round about me. Everything began to shake violently. Dread filled my heart. I braced myself, and suddenly I was hurled out of the darkness into white light. I rolled many times on what felt like soft sand, and lay sprawled for several moments. I slowly rose to my feet as my eyes gradually adjusted.

I looked behind me.

I couldn't believe what I saw.

The biggest whale I'd ever seen was parked near the shore, and he was staring right at me. It was the most surreal thing I had ever seen. Our gazes met, and it seemed he was smiling at me (if a whale could smile, that is). After a few minutes he shot a stream of water out of his blowhole, turned, and leapt back into the sea. I spun around with a dropped jaw as comprehension dawned.

So that's where I've been all this time? Inside that whale? Who would believe it!

I had hardly begun to take it all in when, to my further amazement, I glimpsed from afar the city I thought I'd never see.

Nineveh! How could this be? I thought I had run out of chances, but here I am! Here I am . . . and this time, I'll do it right.

And so I begin to see. I now come to understand that my God is a God of second chances. Although I failed so terribly, He preserved my calling. He knew ahead of time the decisions I would make, and still He chose me. He never gave up on me, even though He could have chosen someone far better. I thought my future was lost for good, but all along He had it safely hid in His heart. He was with me when I took my first rebellious step, and He is with me now. His faithfulness never fails me and His love prevails.

That is the chief thing.

Now, I have passion in my heart. I have a message to proclaim. I have a calling to fulfill.

Leaving footprints of redemption in the sand, I set out for the city and didn't look back.

Fifteen

Dreams

Lord, I can do all things with Your strength. I am nothing without You, but with You nothing will be impossible for me. With You, I can run with the horses. I can mount up with eagle's wings. I can reach the stars.

I do not have strength of arms, but I can win any battle. I have just a sling and a stone, but I can defeat any giant. I am only a flickering candle, but I can bring light to the darkest places.

You have planted Your dreams inside of me. You alone will realize them. You have a plan and a future for me. Only You can perform them. You have started a good work in me. You will be faithful to finish it.

In Your power I can climb the highest

mountain. I can venture the most tempestuous sea. I can run the hardest course. I can endure any storm. Your strength will be perfect in my weakness.

I have no merit, and I don't deserve any of Your plans, but I've found grace in Your heart. I am the worst of the sinners, but I have redemption as I fall at Your feet. My faith is small, but I will be healed when I touch the wounds in Your hands. I have fallen so many times, but You always rescue me with a mighty hand and an outstretched arm. I was worthless, but I am now the crown upon Your head. And although I am a failure, I am still the apple of Your eye.

You choose the foolish, so choose me. You use the powerless, so use me. You call those who are counted as nothing, so call me, Lord.

Use my hands to feed the hungry and use my feet to bring glad tidings to the poor. Use my voice to declare hope to the broken-hearted and use my eyes to search out the lost. Use my life to beat the darkness and use it as an instrument of light.

No one is too small for You and nothing is too hard for You. You are the God of the miraculous and You are the God of all hope. Your wings will give flight to my dreams and Your promise will be a rock on which I stand. I will not be shaken. I will not be moved.

With You, I can do anything.

Sixteen

A Letter from Humility

Come close child
Listen to my whisper
You will find me in hidden places
I hide deep within the
mines of your soul
I'm the hushed whisper
after the fires burn
I'm the poised silence
when the world trembles
I'm the twinkle for your jaded eyes
The twinkling star
in your downbeat skies
I'm the tumbling tear
from the eye of the defeated
And the sparkle in the
eye of the darkest storm
I'm the stem beneath the blanket of the
lustrous petals of spring
I'm the morning dew on the emerald
blades of sweeping fields

Anthology of a Twenty Year Old Soul

I'll be gone before you're awake
I'm the mysterious ray
reaching from the golden sun
Too dazzling to behold
I'm the star behind the
pink cloud of twilight
My time has not yet come

I'm beauty in disguise
I'm the diminutive core of all that's holy
I'm the shining result
of all those starless nights
I'm the dimple in the
cheek of a sincere smile
I aim to be me
Just who God has called me to be
Unaffected, honest, real, and true
I'll always love you
Just the way God has made you
Pretension, artificiality,
facades, and fake fronts
These are my devilish foes
I'm deeper than skin and show

I never boast and I'll never judge
I'm faithful and loyal and

A Letter from Humility

I never hold a grudge
Forgiveness and compassion are mine
When my back is bleeding
and I've just been stabbed
I won't turn to catch the culprit
I don't care who said it

Look. Can you see me?
I'm the seven-year old on the swing
I'm the daughter dancing alone in the
bedroom for an unseen King
I'm the teenage brother hanging out
with my little sister for the day
I sometimes disagree with my parents
but am quick to obey

Explore. Will you find me?
You might discover me in
places not so sweet
I'm the man with sign in hand
on the heartless street
If the Church is a body,
then I must be the feet
Or the blind left hand while my right
breaks what's wrong
The concealed place of righteousness is

where I belong
You want my coat?
Take my shirt too
Want me to walk with you a while?
For you, I'll go an extra mile

Search. Have you detected me in the
smallest of things?
At Barnes and Noble
There's only one comfortable chair left
Another guy's got his eyes on it
I could easily beat him to it
But I'll leave it alone
Cushions are overrated anyhow

Sprawled out on the floor
as I read my book
My attention is caught by its fantastic plot
But I'm pulled down to reality
when a man calls my name
He approaches me and talks to me
So I'll set down my book
and look him in the eye
Because right now,
he's the most important
person in the world

A Letter from Humility

Gaze. Gaze into my eyes,
the windows of my soul
I'm ripped and broken
I've fought my wars
I know I've fallen flat
I'm flat on the floor
Spent and depleted
My soul is scarred
But my purpose will be completed
So I'll persist for the highest star
I'll persevere so that I'll hear
"Well done, My son,
Well done"

I'm not wanting the applause of men
I perform for an audience of One
My stage is the wooden floor
beneath bent knees
I've lost the world
I've gained my soul
I soar with the eagles
Then play with the children
When the adults are debating
I never know what they're saying
Because I'm the monster on the floor
with three kids on my back

Maybe it's true that good guys finish last
But little does everyone know
Last is my aim
If I'm the very least
I've won the game

Choose me
And in time
You'll be rewarded openly

Seventeen

Narrative of a Crippled Soul

Crippled and still, I lie on my bed. I've been staring at the ceiling for a couple of hours. Initially, I started staring for the first hour or so because I felt I had nothing better to do. For the last hour, though, my boredom has grown into contemplation. And my contemplation has produced discovery.

And my discovery is more costly than gold.

I once was a dreamer. And my dreams were big. I reached for the stars and chased the setting sun, and I knew that the sky was my limit.

I had the whole world ahead of me.

Nothing could stop me and my titanic aspirations.

Nothing at all.

That is, nothing until I received news from my physician. News that I would never walk again.

I remember that day perfectly.

The fateful day I awoke to find all my dreams broken, my desires helplessly slipping through my fingers, and my hope shattered like countless shards of fallen clay pottery.

But today, as I lie here on my bed, I have indeed made a discovery: a vital find both monumental and divine.

Today, I have discovered that the first day of my paralysis may well have been the best day of my life.

See, in the past I was a very wicked man: a wretch driven by lust and pride, a scoundrel given to treachery and deceit, a degenerate immersed in depravity and nefariousness. My heart was cold as ice and hard as stone.

But when I received news that I would never walk again, everything changed.

And only now have I come to understand that that was the day I was rescued from my monstrous condition. That was the day the poison of selfishness flooded out of my system. The day my soaring pride came crashing down.

The day I became a better man.

Beneath the surface of fallen hopes and devastated dreams, there has been hidden treasure that I've not chanced on till today.

Of course, if ever I were to walk again, by some strange miracle, every step taken would leave a footprint of indelible gratitude. Oh, the joy of such thought!

Nevertheless, if I should remain as I am, I will be thankful still. I now understand that my impairment is a blessing, for in it

I've found the treasured lesson of character, an invaluable possession I've never owned.

And something tells me that this is the revelation that will shift the course of my future.

Still, this revelation, monumental as it is, fails to soothe my tormented soul. It's as if a great void lives inside of me that nothing manages to fill.

This void has been a cruel despot that I cannot overthrow.

And I am afraid.

For my greatest fear lies not in the fact that I may never walk again. My greatest fear is that my sins have estranged me from God. My greatest fear is that I will not be forgiven of my crimes. The haunting memory of my wickedness ruthlessly tortures my conscience, threatening me with the flames of hell day and night.

I meander through a solitary darkness, searching in vain to find the way of redemption.

But I am desperately lost.

All of a sudden, my mind's occupation with my despairing situation is quickly disrupted when I hear heavy footsteps and my name being called. Startled, I turn over in my bed to find my four closest friends standing in the doorway. Bent over with hands on knees, their breathing is labored as though they'd just run a mile.

"He's here!" one exclaims nearly out of breath. "The famous Healer has come!"

Unbelieving, I ask, "You mean the Teacher from Nazareth?"

"Yes," he replies, his face beaming. "He's just down the street. We've come to take you to Him!"

Impossible hope rushes into my heart like a thousand cascading waterfalls dashing to the earth below. Could He be the one to rescue me? Is He the one to deliver me from the consuming darkness that has ensnared me?

There is no time to even grant them permission, when they lift me and carry me out the door.

"See, my friend," says one with eyes steadfast ahead, "there is hope for you yet."

With each friend carrying one corner of my bed, they race down the street. We make our way to a small residence a short distance away. I raise my head and see vast crowds besieging the small home. But upon our arrival, we discover that the multitudes block any passage into the house.

There's no way in.

In an attempt to ward off discouragement, I dwell on the hope that my loyal friends will find a way . . . surely they will find a way.

I look up to my friends for assurance, and I find the hope I need. In the eyes of my friend on the far right corner, I recognize that infamous glint of insanity. It's the look he gets whenever he has a crazy idea.

"We're going up," he said evenly. "We're breaking through the roof."

"Breaking through the roof?!" we cried all at once.

"Of course," he replied nonchalantly, as if that were the obvious solution. "Let's go."

With a shrug and a disbelieving laugh from the other three, they carry me up to the roof.

Now, consider the scene: here I am, lying on top of the house of a family I have never met. Below us, Jesus is in the middle of His teaching while my friends begin to noisily pick apart the roof. As the opening slowly grows, pieces of debris drop on unsuspecting members of the crowd. Soft laughter ripples through the overflow of people outside. Bewildered, amused, and annoyed faces turn up at us simultaneously.

And I feel quite ridiculous.

But still, I can't help but admire the reckless faith and dogged loyalty of my friends. Nothing ever keeps them from aiding a person in need. They've always been there for me, and I'd wager they would even give their lives for me if they had to.

Eventually, after all their toilsome digging, they manage a hole just large enough for me and my bed to slip through. They lower me steadily to the ground as the people inside are forced to make way. A wave of protests and gasps pass over the room.

But I don't notice.

In fact, I am entirely unaware of everyone else because the first glimpse of Him wholly captures my attention.

I finally see Jesus.

His physicality is that of any other

Jewish man and His appearance is definitely not what I expected. He just looks so . . . well . . . ordinary. I might even guess He is . . . I don't know . . . maybe a carpenter or something. But it is nothing somatic that overwhelms me. Rather, it is something deeply spiritual, maybe even divine. For His countenance is angelic, His gaze fixed, and His eyes fierce.

I look into those eyes. I gaze into two fathomless oceans of compassion. Those eyes pierce through my very soul.

Captivated, I am unable to speak.

All is silent.

He opens His mouth to speak.

"Son," He says, "your sins are forgiven."

Everything I ever was, everything I could ever hope to be, is lost.

Now I find myself in Him.

I inhale, and an eternity of life fills my soul. My heart beats. My eyes see. My ears hear. And I am born again.

I am new.

The void explodes. The tyrant dies. The war is won.

The silence is broken when a crystal tear shatters on the floor.

That tear is mine.

I lower my gaze to examine it, when a calloused hand gently lifts my chin.

I look upon Him again.

He looks at me, into me, and says, "Rise, take up your bed and walk."

I rise.

I stand.

Tears stream down my face.

And in this miraculous moment, when the swirling winds of my life collide, I am changed forever.

Eighteen

Bridge to Tomorrow

How many todays have I missed because I waited only for the tomorrows? How many new memories haven't been made because I've been trapped in old ones? How many blessings have I taken for granted because I was only concerned with what I didn't have?

Today is the gift You've given me, I'll never have it again, so I'll cherish every breath.

Today is the only bridge to tomorrow, so I'll savor the journey toward my destination.

Tomorrow is an empty canvas with the potential to become a masterpiece, and my present choices decide its fate. What I do today will determine what my tomorrow will be, and who I am right now determines who I am going to be. I will seize the present and I'll aim to reach my full potential. I will build on yesterday's foundation and I will learn from my past.

Life is quickly passing. Today will soon be gone. Now is my chance.

I'll leave my inhibitions behind and my heart will beat with abandon. I will draw breath from eternal skies and I will discover new heights. My voice will sound a hope that's sure and my ears will apprehend Heaven's conversation.

Though sun above may fail and grounds beneath me tremble; though sea ahead may hinder and enemies behind draw nearer; though battles rise without and wars are waged within, I will be brave and triumphant in the strength of the Lord. I will not complain about the hurdles: I will jump over them. I won't get down because the mountains are high: I will scale them. I will not let the giants prevent me from my promised land: I will defeat them.

I'll live today like I have never lived it before, and my purpose will be revealed. I'll grab hold of every minute. I'll press on toward my goals. I'll walk in Your plans. I'll persevere in my course. And I won't look back.

The Kingdom is here. A new day has begun. And while I wait for eternity, eternity waits for me. Eternity hangs on today, today is decided by the moment, and the moment is in my hands. I put my life into this moment and I give it back to You.

Nineteen

Peter's Redemption

"Lord, where are You going?"

"You can't come with Me, Peter. Not this time. But you will follow Me in the end."

"Why can't I come now? I am ready to die for You!"

"Die for Me? No, before the cock crows at dawn tomorrow, you will deny me three times."

"No! Not even if I must die with You. I will never deny You!"

I remember how my heart leaped every time Jesus would say the words: "Peter, let's go for a walk." Some of my best memories were when He and I would converse as we ambled along the shore. Sometimes we talked about the tales of long ago and the inspiring adventures of the characters of Scripture. Other times, we would talk about the future, and even discuss Heaven. But my favorite conversations were when we just talked about life and all that was currently going on. I would tell Him about my problems, and He always managed to solve each one. He was amazingly attentive and keen to hear every word, even when I would prattle on endlessly. He had a way of making me feel like I was the most important person in the world. Whenever I had a question, big or small, He always had just the right answer. When I was down, He would reassure me by speaking of the promises of God. When I was out of line, His firm but tender reproof would quickly put me in my place.

He was a friend who would always be there.

Our most memorable walk was on a brisk spring morning after we breakfasted on the beach. It would be the last before His return to Heaven.

"Peter," He said, "do you love Me more than these?"

I was initially very surprised by the question. It had only been a couple of weeks since I betrayed my love for Him. The wound still festered in my heart . . .

I was sitting outside in the courtyard as Jesus stood before the council. While I warmed myself by the fire, a servant girl approached me and said, "You were one of those with Jesus the Galilean."

Everyone around stared at me with uniform inquisitive gazes.

"I have no idea what you're talking about," I said unflinchingly. "I do not even know the Man!"

"Yes, Lord," I said at last. "You know that I love You."

"Then feed My lambs."

We walked in silence for a moment as I considered His question. Occasionally during our walks we wouldn't speak for some time, content merely to be in each other's company.

"Peter," He said again, "do you love Me?"

Everyone was whispering and gaping at me.

"Why can't they just leave me alone?" I thought to myself, so I left where I was sitting and stood next to the gate. I draped my hood over my head and did my best to keep to myself, when a wide-eyed girl began to inch toward me. She looked me up and down, then shouted suddenly.

"I know him! He followed Jesus!" she said, her little finger pointed at me.

Droplets of sweat trickled down my flushed face. "I have never associated myself with that Man!" I said angrily.

"I told you I don't even know Him. I'm telling the truth . . . I swear it!"

"Yes, Lord," I said with my head bowed in shame, "You know that I love You."

Jesus put His hand on my shoulder and gently replied, "Then take care of My sheep."

My eyes moistened as we continued on in silence. His gracious words never ceased to astonish me. My love for the Man I denied collided with a concurrent hatred of the traitor I'd become. Surging emotions swirled wildly inside me as I fought back the tears with all the strength I could muster.

"Peter, do you love Me?" Jesus asked a third time.

"Your voice betrays you!" countered a large man with a gruff voice. "You have a Galilean accent. Surely you are one of them!"

"No!" I said cowering. "No! I swear by God I do not know the Man!"

At that moment a tumultuous crowd stormed into the courtyard drawing the Lord in fetters. They mercilessly spit on and struck His blood-stained face. A raging malice reverberated from the vociferous mob as they hurled their injurious curses and insults upon Him. He deliberately lifted His head and looked upon me with love.

Our eyes locked.

A rooster sounded a piercing cry in the distance. I turned and hurried outside. I fell to my knees in my despair, buried my head in my hands, and wept.

An unimpeded stream of tears spilled down my face. "Yes Lord!" I cried. "You know all things! You know that I love You!"

A light sparkled in His eyes as He turned to face me. He put His scarred hands on my shoulders and said, "Then feed My sheep."

For an eternal moment I lost myself in the depths of His gaze. His eyes revealed absolute forgiveness and unconditional love. Sudden understanding emerged like a thousand stars appearing at nightfall: I have been redeemed. Three times I denied Him before, and three times I confess Him now. I am forgiven.

Twenty

Hope to the End

Has despair seized your heart? Do you feel like lying down and never getting back up? Has hope become to you but a misled optimism or an illusory expectation? Have you discontinued your once dauntless and child-like faith in God's promises? Have you abandoned your dreams as you resign yourself to a fate abiding in sorrow? Do you believe happy endings are only a myth? Is tomorrow's light swallowed by the shadows cast by today? Has the journey taken a devastating toll? Do you travel feeling alone and forlorn as if God is no longer by your side?

You cannot stare down the lion for much longer. He stalks to and fro, slowly tearing down your last defense in courage.

His menacing eyes pierce your soul like cold blades. He crouches for his final blood-thirsty attack. He sounds a malevolent roar as if to summon a storm of fury, and waits for the subsequent foreboding silence to fill the air. All is still. Then, with a fatal spring, he unleashes his rage as you recoil in horror.

In this moment, at the pinnacle of hopelessness and fear, God dispatches a messenger of hope: an angel descends with fire and sword, shielding you with an impregnable cover of light. The mighty lion, thrown into sudden madness, crashes help-lessly to the earth. He draws back trembling. Defeated, he turns and flees in retreat.

The tyrant is overthrown. Your chains are broken. Freedom is won.

You've been kept at bay by this ruth-less demon for too long. He's spoken cease-less despair to your growing emptiness, seeking only to complete your progression towards utter ruination. Like a lingering fear, his presence has hovered over your mind, crippling you slowly.

But today you are victorious. The void is closing. A new hope rises.

Lift your eyes and set out for the horizon. Take hold of the promises of God. Follow your dreams. When you fall, don't stay down. Get up and persevere for God's plans. Courageously wait for Him, and He will strengthen you. Delight yourself in Him, and He will give you your heart's desires. Stand firm and never give up.

Flowers cannot grow without the rain. The rain in your life gives you beauty and strength. But flowers also cannot grow without the sun. God knows you need brighter days, and brighter days are ahead. So blossom right where you are. Grow where you're planted. Welcome every season; you need each one.

You can't get to spring without winter.

Anthology of a Twenty Year Old Soul

You can't reach the light without first going through the tunnel. You can't see the stars without the night, and you can't get to the dawn without the darkness. Without darkness, you will never truly understand light. Without sorrow in the night, you will never truly value the joy that comes in the morning. Without great difficulties, there are no great deeds. Without battle, there can be no victory. Without loss, there can be no virtue.

Maybe there are simple answers to complex problems. Perhaps tomorrow does make sense of today. Aren't happy endings always built on foundations of trouble? Could there be a good story without catastrophe in the plot? Don't tears of joy fall on the final page because tears of grief have stained the tragic middle pages?

This is your story. Even now it is being written. Your character is being built, and what you do with this page determines what the next page will be. Will yours be a tale of courage in adversity? Valor and strength? Perseverance despite peril and danger? Belief to overcome impossible odds? Resistance until victory?

Stand your ground. Be strong. Hope to the end.